Spot 12

FIVE MONTHS IN THE NEONATAL ICU

JENNY JAECKEL

❀ Raincloud Press

Chico, California

For Asa and Chris

Spot 12

© 2016 Jenny Jaeckel

ISBN 978-1-941203-11-8

Printed in the United States of America

Published by Raincloud Press

www.raincloudpress.com

raincloudpress@gmail.com

Library of Congress Control Number: 2016945504

Book design: Josué Menjivar, www.freshbrewedillustration.com

Cover design by Josué Menjivar and Raincloud Press

contact the author: spot12book@gmail.com

author blog: www.jennyjaeckel.com

Spot12

FIVE MONTHS IN THE NEONATAL ICU

JENNY JAECKEL

I had a normal pregnancy right up until the end. But in the last couple of weeks I started getting much bigger than normal and the midwives sent me to have an ultrasound.

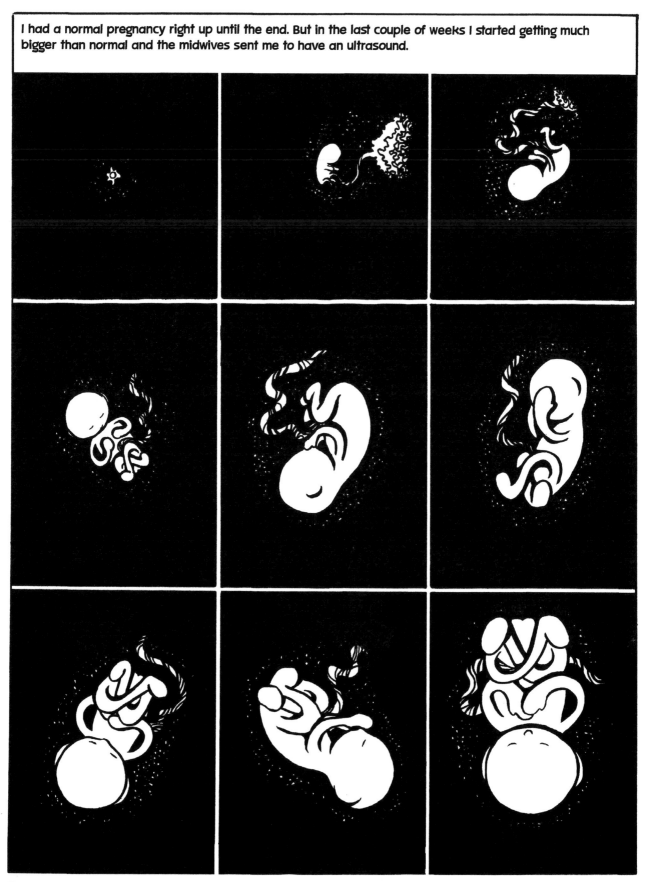

I had the ultrasound at a clinic on a Saturday and they found I had excess amniotic fluid. They told me there was a 40 percent chance there was a problem with the baby, but they didn't see anything wrong, except for the baby's abdomen looking small.

I asked the technician if she could tell the gender. I couldn't believe it when she said a girl. I'd wanted a girl so badly. I asked a few times if she was certain, and she said, "Yep, those are labia."

On Monday our midwife, M. Corduroy, met us at the hospital for a more detailed ultrasound and to get advice from a neonatologist. They told us there were too many risks to have a home birth as we'd planned, or even wait to go into spontaneous labor. At 38 weeks, it was better to induce the labor in the hospital that same day

M. Corduroy found that I was already between one and two centimeters dilated, which was favorable for being induced. I was admitted, met with an obstetrician and was taken to a delivery room.

Cito and M. Corduroy went back to our apartment and got the bag I'd packed. I lay on a mat on the floor and made a phone call.

I had a phone tree a friend had set up. I wanted the good thoughts of everyone who loved me. Cito and Corduroy returned, the nurse came in, and the process began.

Gowned and monitored, they had me slump on the edge of the bed for my epidural. I prayed for guidance from above, and support from below, as the feeling went out of my legs.

I was strapped to the bed, it was my lifeboat heading into the deepening night.

Hours later they wheeled me into the OR to drain the excess fluid. Everyone was in scrubs and shower caps, including Cito and the two midwives, M. Cotton and her assistant, who had come to replace M. Corduroy. Under blinding lights, we waited. When the doctor came she broke the sac and the amniotic fluid began draining into a bucket somewhere below. It drained and drained and relieved the pressure against my ribs. Normally a woman has about a liter of fluid at term; I had eight. The shape of the baby became visible beneath my skin.

HOLY TOLEDO!

IT'S AN OCEAN!

Back to delivery. I was wailing and bracing my hands against the bed rails. Cito spoke encouragement but I was scarcely aware of him. This was hour fourteen of the labor. The head descended. The doctor came back. They told me to start pushing.

GET THE DOCTOR!

Blacking out, oxygen mask, M. Cotton told me when to breathe, push, tuck my chin. I heard their urgency and I concentrated entirely on pushing. The doctor was busy at my vagina. The placenta was tearing away too soon. Blood poured out of me. The baby's heart rate was dropping

And then she was out, whisked across the room, making a strange noise, not a cry. A buzz, a rattle. I tried to ask if she was ok.

The delivery room door was wide open and more people were rushing in and out. I asked to have the door shut, and Cotton said, "They're here for the baby."

They swooped her over to me. I saw her pale face, closed eyes, a little flared nose. Briefly, she opened her eyes and looked at me. I couldn't tell if she was breathing. "Give her a kiss!" someone said. Then they disappeared out the door with Cito running behind.

Someone asked Cito if he wanted to put on the hat that would make her a real Canadian.

The nurses worked quietly. The clock said eleven in the morning. Then twelve.

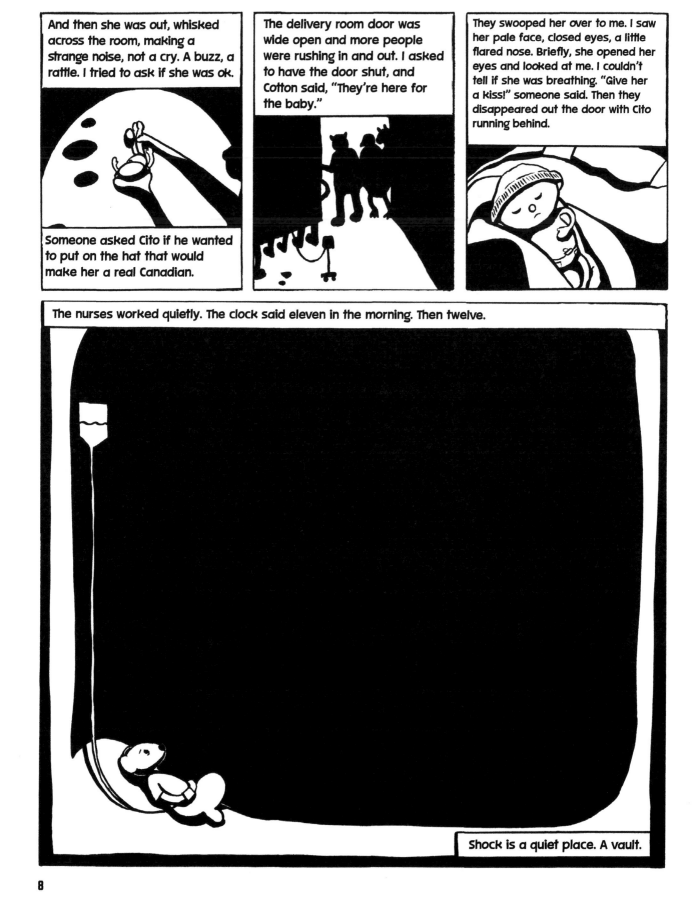

Shock is a quiet place. A vault.

The pediatrician came back to the room to explain what they thought was wrong. But she was far across the room and the oxygen mask had a loud hiss. I couldn't understand a word.

The midwives seemed miles away and then faded out. There was a phone call from "my sister." It was Midwife Friend Deer.

The nurses went off shift, and were replaced with new ones. I asked one of them, "Do you think she'll be ok?" She said, "I don't know." I was empty, cold. Her answer was echoing, bottomless.

In the next few hours Cito went back and forth between the Neonatal Intensive Care Unit (NICU) and my bed. Then I was transferred to a hospital room.

They told Cito the baby had a problem with her esophagus and trachea. Babies actually regulate the amount of amniotic fluid in the uterus by drinking it. Our baby wasn't able to swallow much and that's why the fluid kept building up. This could be repaired surgically, they said, and they would operate the same day.

We named her quickly: Asa from a list of Hebrew names, meaning 'healer'. That was it. And Eve, as a middle name, after my grandmother.

Room 41

Where was she?

Neonatal Intensive Care Unit

Room 41

Spot 12

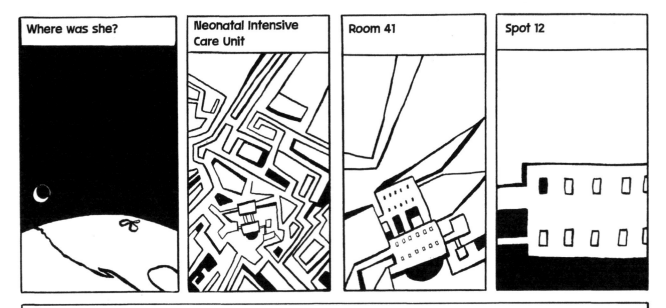

The second time I saw Asa was before the surgery. I tried to stand up and looked for a place to touch her, this wretched, half-dead-looking tiny stranger who was our baby.

A doctor in scrubs began describing a procedure where part of the intestines are relocated outside the body. Did this have something to do with us? I tried to pay attention, but I was feeling faint.

In my room we called our parents in California and Philadelphia to tell them what was happening. And then we waited.

Hours later, one of the surgeons, Dr. Strideforth, came to my room and told us the operation went well. He thought Asa would need two or three weeks in the hospital to recover. It was unfathomable that we'd have to stay so long. We'd never intended to come at all.

I was a hospital patient for five days. Cito slept on a mat on the floor.

I had lost a lot of blood and I fainted on the toilet.

Slowly I came out of shock and into the cold grip of fear: The agony of seeing my child in pain, in danger, in isolation, the confusion of this turn of events.

The night of the birth I'd slept an hour, the next night about three.

They were heating her with lamps. She had a catheter because swelling prevented her from peeing, so except for the instruments she was naked. Despite everything, she was lovely, and so tiny. Though big for the NICU, five pounds five ounces, precisely my own birth weight. It was a clue she belonged to me.

After the surgery Asa's condition was unstable. The nurse wouldn't say much, just, "She kept me very busy last night."

The nurse laid a soft hand on my arm. She said women broke down even where there was nothing wrong with the baby. She brought me two tablets to help me sleep.

Cito came into the room with a cup that had some of Asa's hair in it. They had shaved part of her head in order to access a vein. I saw wisps of dark fur. I held onto the cup and slept a little.

Exhaustion made me less able to sleep. I heard other babies crying in the rooms next to mine or out in the hall with their mothers. I wanted her. I only knew I wasn't with her.

In the morning, a psychiatrist asked me a lot of questions and gave me a prescription for more pills. Supposedly they were safe to take while lactating.

DID YOU HAVE A HAPPY CHILDHOOD?

Later somebody said, "Don't be alarmed, it's not as bad as it looks."

Most of the babies in Room 41 were premature and locked up in aquariums. One nurse to two patients. Fluorescent lights glared, screens everywhere, ventilators, feeding and IV pumps, two telephones, sinks running, streams of people coming in and out, shouting. Asa would be asleep and someone would shout right next to her.

Cito's brother Dill flew in from Philadelphia.

I stayed with Asa as much as I could but I was still very weak. I learned how to use the breast pump and Cito put the colostrum in the NICU deep freeze, since Asa couldn't have any food yet.

My mom arrived from California. From the bed I saw her walk in.

She brought some things we needed from our apartment and a bunch of purple flowers we'd received from the world we had suddenly departed.

My mom took a picture of Asa that I later taped to the foot of my bed. In it she was swollen from the surgery, and in the middle of all the wires was a gold color foil heart.
I tried to see these as instruments of love.

I don't believe anyone used the term "birth defect." They said, "anomalies." I couldn't shake the feeling that I was, we were, contaminated.

Piece by piece, we understood that Asa was born with a "tracheoesophageal fistula" (TEF) and "esophageal atresia" —a malformed esophagus.

mouth

The top part of her esophagus ended in a pocket rather than continuing on to her stomach.

And then from her stomach up was a section of esophagus which had been attached to the wrong place. Her trachea. This wrong connection was the tracheoesophageal fistula.

esophagus

Trachea

esophagus

lungs

Stomach

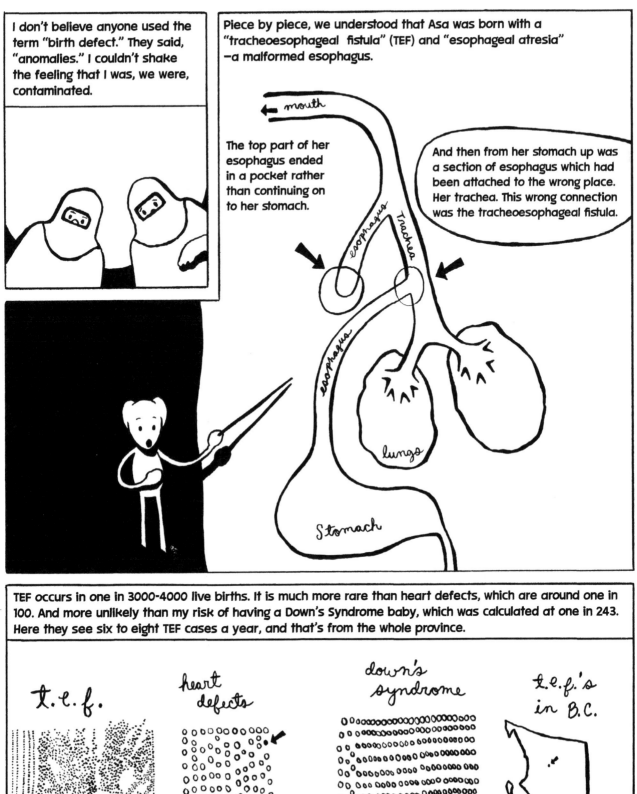

TEF occurs in one in 3000-4000 live births. It is much more rare than heart defects, which are around one in 100. And more unlikely than my risk of having a Down's Syndrome baby, which was calculated at one in 243. Here they see six to eight TEF cases a year, and that's from the whole province.

t. e. f.

heart defects

down's syndrome

t.e.f.'s in B.C.

How had this happened? I had the complete organic pregnancy. I walked the other way if I smelled a cigarette or a molecule of house paint. Yet something had interfered with the normal development of her anatomy around week six of Asa's gestation.

I read that birth defects are on the rise and are the number one killer of infants in the United States.

(*Having Faith, An Ecologist's Journey to Motherhood* by Dr. Sandra Steingraber, 2001)

At some point, I noticed a sign in Radiology that warned pregnant women not to enter, and someone told me that this amount of radiation was equal to riding in an airplane. I'd been on a plane around week six of pregnancy, and when I asked Dr. Storytime about it he said, "It only takes one particle."

One particle is not hard to come by.

They told us there were other potential problems associated with TEF: Defects of the heart, the kidneys, the spine. They would need to do more tests.

After I was discharged, Cito and I moved into the Haunter House, a sort of hostel for patients' families. It had a communal kitchen, and a shared bathroom with a tub. The room had a sealed window that looked out onto a delivery area.

My mom stayed at our apartment and we fell into a rough routine. I was on the breast pump every three hours, and had to eat and drink a lot to keep it up. Eating and pumping took about eight hours a day, time that took me away from Asa.

After two weeks, Cito went back to school. He stopped his coursework but continued his work as a teaching assistant. He needed to be on campus two days a week, and also had papers to mark. The three of us worked out rotating shifts with Asa, from early in the morning until late at night. Cito and I hardly saw each other.

The nurses were always there. But their concern was to keep her alive, not comfortable. They were busy with their other patients, their notes, meetings, breaks and so on.

I didn't see my mom much either, though that may have been for the best since often we didn't get along. Cito and I desperately needed help, and she was willing to do it, but having her close was dreadful for me.

There were times of solidarity, but things went badly for us
when I was still very small.

My mom helped a lot. It was amazing what she could get done in a day. In addition to helping Asa,

She shopped,

She cooked,

She did errands and brought us things from home.

She went swimming every morning at the community center,

She sent emails,

DEAR FRIENDS

She attended a meditation group,

And prepared platters of snacks for the nurses, a pie on my birthday.

She made friends everywhere she went.

COME BACK SOON!

THANKS FOR THE TEE SHIRT!

Contention between us was inevitable and germs were one thing. Infection is a huge danger in intensive care. Anything that fell on the floor either went straight into the laundry or the garbage. My mom washed her hands before going into the unit but paying attention to germs wasn't something she was used to. Sometimes she picked up things off the floor, and then touched Asa's soother.

Cito and I asked her to wash her hands more and she felt criticized. She felt all we did was nag her for not washing her hands.

These were our first days of being parents and we had so little access to Asa. There were so many strangers in her life, whether we wanted them there or not. We could make so few decisions for her. So these disagreements loomed large and at times my mom and I were barely speaking.

I was still weak, I had a fair amount of pain and my sutures became infected. And I was incontinent which didn't help at all. Once when I couldn't move fast enough I pooped in my pants and once I pooped on the floor. Could I have given birth out of my butt? M. Corduroy said, "Yes, the anus stretches as much as the vagina." I'd read a pile of birth books and not one had mentioned that!

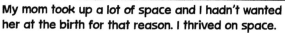

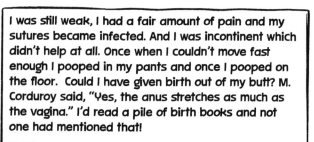

I had little time with Asa and I was possessive of it. It was good to be there with Cito part of the time, because I missed him. But I asked my mom to let me have time alone with Asa. But she often barged back in after five or ten minutes.

My mom took up a lot of space and I hadn't wanted her at the birth for that reason. I thrived on space.

When Asa was awake we talked and sang to her softly. We weren't able to hold her but we kept a hand resting on her lightly.

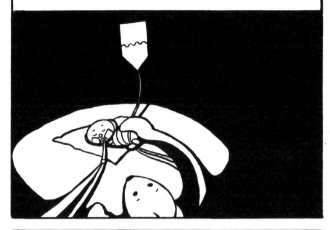

We started to learn the hospital lingo, the meaning of the numbers on the monitor that was tracking her oxygen levels, her respiration and heart rate, which beep meant what.

HER SATS ARE LOW.

SHE HAD T.P.N. AND SHE'S STILL N.P.O.

She cried when she was stuck with needles for new IV sites, went for procedures, etc. But otherwise she was surprisingly alert and calm.

We realized quickly that when she was agitated and upset there was something really wrong. One afternoon she writhed and cried until the nurse finally figured out that one of her lungs had collapsed over the drainage tube from her surgery.

You see the pain and fear in her face and are helpless. It makes you want to scream. So you do, into the pillow, late at night, on the phone with your friend.

They first tried to take her off the ventilator when she was three days old. She was able to breathe on her own for a couple of hours, but then she got too tired to breathe effectively and they had to put her back on the ventilator. Something was obstructing her airway.

Being on a ventilator doesn't allow any air to pass through the vocal chords, which means the voice can't be heard. Those hours off ventilation, her voice was hoarse from being irritated by the tube, but after a while we did hear her voice the tiniest bit, a couple of high little notes.

Extubation, tube out, is pretty easy, but intubation, tube in, is difficult, and Asa turned out to be especially difficult to intubate. It took several people and had to be done quickly or she would asphyxiate.

Asa had a number of other procedures. She had ink injected into her nose under xray to check the surgical repairs and make sure there were no leaks. There were a number of sonograms.

Her heart was normal. So were her kidneys and spine.

When a week had passed they tried extubating again, without success. Two days later, during the night, Asa extubated herself by pulling away from the tube. She was alone after the intubation with no one to comfort her.

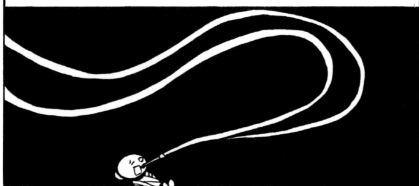

As the days went by, they still hadn't figured out why Asa couldn't breathe on her own.

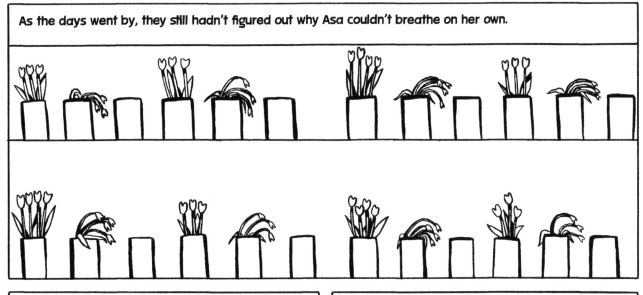

She underwent a series of scopes, and more trial extubations.

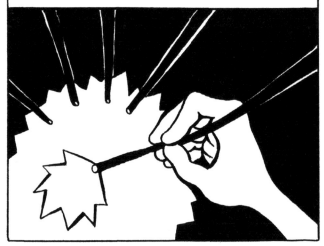

They prepared Asa for every scope with high doses of a steroid to reduce the inflammation in her airway. This aided in the scope and increased the possibility of a successful extubation. However, the steroid could interfere with organ development, and also the brain.

The scopes were done in the OR under general anesthesia, which had its own risks and side effects, and meant more IVs and no food for several hours prior. Asa returned bruised and puffy, and she cried sometimes for a long time. We told her she was safe.

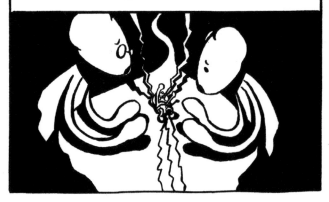

They examined her vocal cords in one of these, having told us that if the cords didn't move, it would mean something was wrong with her brain. Getting the vocal cords to move meant they had to wake her in the middle of the procedure and let her cry. But the cords did move.

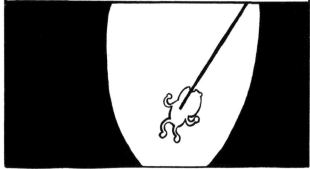

M. Corduroy came to the Haunter House for a postpartum visit when Asa was about 10 days old. After my checkup we talked a bit about the birth.

In the period after the birth, with Asa and Cito gone, the midwives had seemed detached. Corduroy explained that they weren't used to handling emergency situations. I said the nurses had been busy doing I don't know what, and Corduroy said, "They were keeping you from dying." Up to then, I hadn't thought about the birth much because of Asa, but once she said it, I knew it was true.

Later that night, the danger that I myself had been in, hit me in a deep wave of fear. I began to shake and I thought the walls might fall down as I sat there on the bed.

Either it was too late to call Deer, who was on the East Coast, or else I thought I'd already called her too much. I tried a couple of crisis lines but I couldn't talk and just hung up. Then I thought about the clinic where I'd worked. I tried calling Tune, a former coworker, because I felt I suddenly needed a mental health professional.

Tune was at home and once I started talking to her she was so kind and understanding I kept talking, and cried and cried. And after a while I felt more calm. The death fear from the birth never came back in the same way.

My mom brought over some colored pens that could write on glass. I put my prayers on the window because it was a link to the sky—they could fly out and seek help. I hadn't done much praying in my life, but this seemed a fitting way.

Around this time Asa got switched from an oral to a nasal ventilation tube. This was less irritating for her and finally she could suck on something. Certain magazines will tell you that a soother is under no circumstances beneficial to a child. Previously I might have agreed; now it was one of the things I was most thankful for.

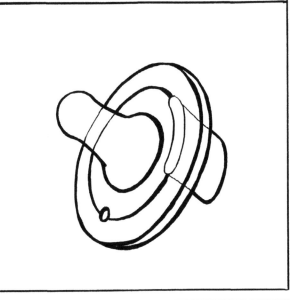

We kept Asa swaddled most of the time at first to make her feel secure and to keep her hands from yanking out the tubes. I loved changing her diaper, it was the only time I really got to handle her, feel her little legs and feet, see her whole body.

Asa got a feeding tube, also nasal, so now she had a tube in each nostril and tape all over her face, but she also could now get real food, the colostrum from the freezer, and then breast milk, rather than whatever it was she'd been getting via IV.

Helpful Hints
for
BREAST PUMPING
in a
Highly Specific SITUATION

Buy a breast pump if you can afford it and keep it by your bed for easy and odd-hour access. Or go to the hospital's pump room as is most convenient.

Use the bags of sterilized pump parts on the hospital pump. Clean before and after as directed. Place used parts in recycle bin for sterilization, label milk and place in fridge or freezer.

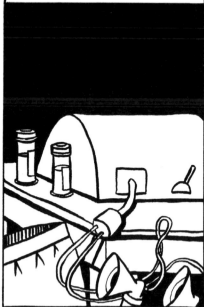

Since pump parts must be sterilized after use (six times per day) and your time is limited, use hospital parts with your own pump.

Unfortunately, this is against the rules and parts must be exchanged by stealth. Bring your used parts to recycle and load up your backpack with bags of clean parts to stow away in a locker. TIP: Go first thing in the morning when no one is likely to be around. Then pull the old 'switcharoo.'

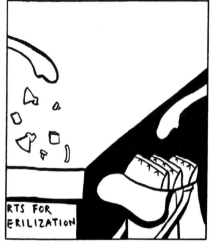

RTS FOR ERILIZATION

Hopefully you will be lucky like me to have enough milk. Lots of women have trouble getting enough using the pump, and go on medication to produce more. For incredible production, you could try, like Lily, a special broth she always drank made from black chickens from Chinatown. Maybe, like her, you will be the talk of the pump room.

Suctioning 101

An Endotracheal (ET) tube for ventilation is a foreign body that causes the human body to produce mucus in an attempt to rid the human body of the foreign body.

The mucus must be cleared using a suction device so the patient can breathe. In Asa's case this had to be done numerous times per day and night.

Some nurses and RTs (Respiratory Therapists) are good at suctioning. Others are inexperienced and ineffective or rough handlers of the suction device.

Rough handling caused Asa major discomfort.

Too much suctioning leads to more mucous secretion and more suctioning, which leads to irritation and possible damage to the delicate tracheal tissue.

Sometimes the mucus is pink from blood and this can be dangerous.

Not enough, or inefficient suctioning causes the blood level of oxygen saturation, Asa's "SATs," to go down. This is called "De-SATing."

Assessing the need for a suction is difficult. One must continually listen to the patient's breathing, observe if she is agitated, review the numbers on the monitor that indicates the SATs and decide whom to ask to suction her. If the nurse that day is not a good suctioner, wait until she is busy and then try to flag down an RT.

As a parent in the NICU you are always watching the SATs. The lower they get, the more afraid you are.

One day Asa's SATs were low. Normally she was in the high 90s and her SATs had dropped into the 80s. She was tossing and crying, agitated in a way that reminded me of her lung collapse.

I was doing my best to comfort her, but the nurse didn't want me touching her. She'd been telling us not to touch her for two days. Then she said it was me that was causing Asa to de-SAT.

Outraged, I went and talked to the charge nurse, who got our nurse reassigned. Soon after, an RT suctioned Asa properly, her SATs went back up and she calmed down.

But the touching was an issue.

Touching her the way we did helped her to sleep. This was apparent if you took the time to look.

Some of the nurses encouraged us to participate in changing Asa's clothes and diaper, take her temperature and clean her eyes. They answered our questions and listened. Others seemed irritated by our presence there. Wanting to participate versus giving them their professional space was often a line of little egg shells.

One nurse even kept telling us to go out and go to the movies, to take the weekend off, a long weekend. We were exhausted and she could see it. But leave Asa alone with her machines and procedures for three days? Was she mad?

CATCH THE FLICKS!

There were a number of nurses who were particularly skilled and kind.

N. Bright

N. Sure

N. Tellme

N. Gentlediaper

Our favorite was N. Chuckles

He was a wealth of knowledge, always offering to help us learn to take care of her. He called her "little person" and treated her that way.

One time Chuckles had Cito help him give Asa a bath. It's not easy to bathe an infant on a ventilator. Chuckles said, "When you go home you'll be doing this, when you go home you'll be doing that." That gave us a lot of hope.

Every couple of days the RTs had to redo the tape on Asa's face that held the ET tube in place. We had to either keep her hands wrapped against her body or put socks on them, or else she would try to pull out the tube with her hands. If the tube slipped even a centimeter, either from loose tape or during the retaping when all the tape was off, she could loose her air supply.

Asa cried having all that tape ripped off her face and new adhesive and tape applied. One time one of the nurses told me to leave for the retaping. When I went back in, Asa's face was blotchy and her eyes were swollen shut from hard crying. I was furious I had obeyed the nurse, because when we were there helping to hold her and talk her through it, she cried some but she stayed pretty calm.

After that we always helped with the retaping. Once when I asked the RTs to let me help hold her and talk to her through it one of them said, "Of course, she's your baby." I loved him for that.

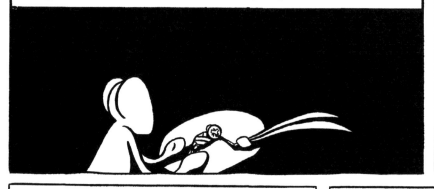

The attitude of the staff seemed generally divided in this way. Hands off vs. Hands on.

My friend Share came to visit. I wanted to cover Asa's head and Share said, "Trust your instincts."

Share was the one person to say this to me and I was grateful for it.

Asa was around two weeks old and she was recovered enough for us to hold her, but only for short periods and not every day. I got to hold her the most at first. I pumped and ate and drank as much as I could beforehand.

On my way to the unit I was like a kid going to a birthday party. I had to wait for the nurse to be ready and an RT to be available to move her and all the tubing, and once it was in place I couldn't get up or move around. By then I had about two hours before I had to pump again.

Asa often cried when she was moved. But once I was holding her she opened her eyes and fixed her gaze on my face in a way she almost never did from the bed.

Bit by bit we got to know some of the other parents in the unit.

Magnolia had premature twins, one of them with undiagnosed breathing problems.

Dahlia's premature son had breathing and other problems.

Aster's son was born at term but with a muscle disease so rare no one on the staff had heard of it. They weren't sure if it was degenerative or not.

LET'S GO SEE YOUR BROTHER.

The Calas' daughter also had a number of issues. She had a tracheostomy and was transferred to another unit.

As with Aster's son, there seemed to be all kinds of new diseases and new birth defects that were affecting babies.

I'VE BEEN HER 18 YEARS AND I'VE NEVER SEEN A BABY BORN WITH A MASS ON HER EPIGLOTTIS

Most babies left the NICU alive, but not all, including some of Asa's neighbors from Spots 11 and 10.

R. didn't make it.

Neither did T.

There was a pair of 23-week-old twins that lasted just the night.

W. was alive but almost never had a visitor, only his disabled grandfather who came twice a week.

It was helpful to be around the other parents. We'd all fallen off the edge of the known world and into the same boat.

Every time I started to feel sorry for myself someone told me about their daughter's severe chromosomal abnormality, or their son with cystic fibrosis or possibly fatal heart defect or brain damage. How could I not be thankful that Asa had every chance of going home? Though that too we couldn't take for granted.

In the parent lounge there were photo albums of babies that had left the NICU with their stories handwritten or typed alongside the pictures. Most of them were success stories about premature babies and their many-months-long journeys through infections and lung disease. Some were memorials. There was an infant born with all his organs outside his body. He lived only a week or two.

This mutual understanding was valuable but it had a heavy price. Our individual crisis was part of a collective one, and the longer we were there I felt more sickened than comforted.

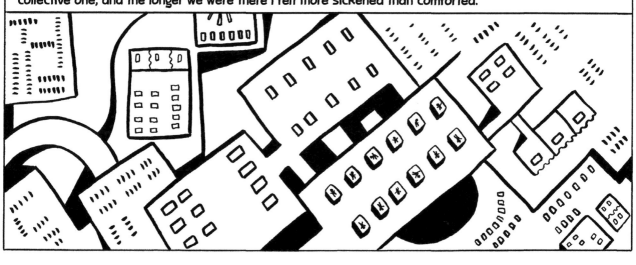

Asa was 20 days old. Cito and I went for a walk outside, and on the ground I found a playing card, the three of hearts. Long before, I once found a miniature playing card in an alley, also the three of hearts. It was the day Cito and I had been together three years. That was an uncertain day and so was this. Cito said this was the three of us and that the hole in the middle was Asa's airway. Our world turned around this point.

There were more scopes, more procedures. By the end of February, they had determined that Asa had "Tracheomalacia," which meant her trachea was too soft, collapsible like a wet straw, something that usually accompanies TEF.

They weren't sure how severe it was or if that was the only issue. They decided to wait two weeks before another scope, to let the swelling come down.

Physically I was challenged. I had had infections, back pain from the epidural, blocked milk ducts and some fevers. Treating, soaking, unblocking, etc. all took up time.

Sometimes I'd lose a day or two when I wasn't allowed in the NICU because of a fever. My dreams of being a parent hadn't included being away like this. Logically I knew it would be counterproductive to visit her while contagious. But I felt like a monster.

I didn't know if Asa could distinguish me from any of the other caregivers. I almost hoped she didn't, so she wouldn't despair when I was gone.

I was exhausted. I slept little, even with the pills. When I did sleep I had nightmares. Once I dreamed I'd given birth to a plastic doll. I'd gone through all those months of pregnancy and the birth, and all I had for it was a dingy, half-broken doll.

When I was with Asa I talked to her. When I was away I did too.

trust we are together even when we're not

We signed the consent for the next scope. If things looked good they might try extubating, and if not they would take advantage of her being under the anesthetic to do a tracheostomy. That is, cut a hole in her neck and insert a plastic tube for her to breathe through. This was a way of getting her off the ventilator and would prevent permanent damage to her trachea from scarring.

She came back from the OR without a tracheostomy but still intubated. Instead the surgical team suggested another surgery, an Aortopexy, a rare operation that had something to do with sewing part of her aorta to her sternum in order to take pressure off her trachea. The trachea would have more room and the hope was that then the collapsibility would be less of an issue, and she'd be able to breathe on her own.

The day before the Aortopexy the head surgeon, Dr. Sofa, came by Asa's bedside when I was alone with her, to explain some of the risks.

We lived in a zone with a wrecking ball. In the beginning it came out of nowhere, but now I often saw it coming.

First I heard the chain creak, then I'd start to feel I was choking, then the impact.

Then there was rubble and the efforts to pull myself back together.

As Dr. Sofa began telling us the seriousness of the operation I felt the wrecking ball's imminent approach. Possibly the nerve controlling her breathing could be damaged. It could take a couple of weeks to be sure, one way or the other. She was also at risk of hemorrhage, though he was careful not to use that word.

THESE ARE THINGS YOU NEED TO KNOW.

That night Cito and I called friends and family to ask for another round of prayers. I put mine on the window.

Marching forward

When your child is going to have a surgery first you must wait for them to set the date, and then you wait for the date to arrive.

The night before you watch the clock and try to sleep.

You get up extra early to be with her beforehand, talk to her, tell her you love her, tell her she's going into another room and to go to sleep, that she's safe, that it's necessary and that all her angels and protectors are with her.

The OR makes the call to the unit, the nurses prep her, you walk with her, see her eyes look for you as they take her through the doors.

STAFF ONLY BEYOND THIS POINT

You have to let your baby go, into the hands of the surgeons, and her own destiny, whatever that is.

When you have a child you give birth to your own heart. Your own heart goes under the knife.

Sometimes Asa fought the hands manipulating her this way and that. She turned beet red and went wild, pawing the air with all four limbs and screaming her voiceless ventilated scream. It was both beautiful and frightening.

She cried this way during her prep. She screamed, she fought, red fire

They told us the surgery would take around two hours. Cito and I went outside to wait. We tried to find a place to sit down but every surface was filthy.

This time I didn't have the luxury of being in shock. I wasn't a big believer in angels or spirits, but I tried to keep a picture in my mind of Asa in the OR with the surgical team surrounding her with an inner circle of angels or guiding spirits, or protective spirits, or the spirit of Cito's mother or my grandmother. Anyone who was available. I prayed that God or whatever would guide the surgical instruments and that it would be a sacred space, and that Asa would be protected, and that she would come through.

After an hour and a half we went back to the parent lounge outside the NICU and continued waiting with my mom and our friend Loo who was up from California. We got a message from reception that the surgery was going "fabulously" but it was taking longer, and it would take another hour or two.

Finally Dr. Sofa arrived. The operation was successful, with no nerve damage and little bleeding.

Cito and I were allowed to go in and see Asa. I was unprepared for what I saw. She looked like she'd been run over by a truck. She was swollen and cut up. She had an arc of bloody sutures under her neck.

Her mouth was frothing from the morphine and she was paralyzed by the drug they used to keep patients still. She smelled of blood and chemicals.

Share came again and held her hands over Asa. She brought up the strong earth energy for Asa's healing.

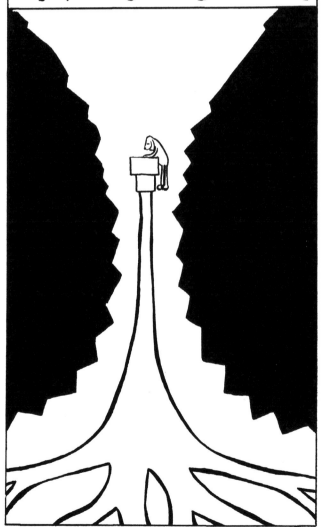

Post-op is a critical period, especially the first 24 to 72 hours. She was closely monitored, her care more detailed. We were lucky N. Bright was on with her. The second day she told me I could touch Asa's feet through the towel covering them, and later took Asa's picture with the unit's "Uniroid."

They gave Asa a vial of blood. I thought, bless this blood and the donor.

Asa's eyes looked out of her swollen face. I looked at her thinking she didn't know she looked grotesque. Her innocence was the most devastating thing of all.

After seven days we could hold her again. She still looked like she'd been through a lot, but babies recover amazingly fast. Asa had new scars to go with her old ones. Cito called them her warrior marks.

Since moving her was so difficult, we began holding Asa in relays. I would hold her for two or three hours, until I had to pump, and then Cito or my mom would take my place in the chair. This way Asa could be held for five or six hours at a time.

Doctors Littlebox, Sofa and Strideforth came to talk to us after the next scope. They said they were happy with the results, Asa was breathing on her own, "like a rose." I jumped up and hugged all three of them.

But back in the NICU Asa started breathing harder, which put too much strain on her trachea, and she was reintubated. They tried again four days later and that extubation also failed. Was the surgery for nothing? Suddenly, I hated them.

After a few more days they did another scope and found a mass of granulation tissue in Asa's trachea, a lumpy pre-scar tissue from the irritation of the ET tube, and this was also obstructing her airway. Dr. Littlebox used laser surgery to burn away the granulation tissue. Asa cried herself beet red and clawed the bed afterward, fell asleep, cried and clawed the bed, for hours.

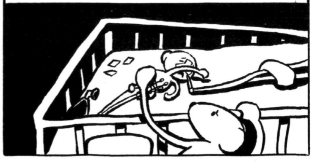

The hospital was crawling with little pairs that could be called "Harmful-and-Helpful," dancing around in bottles and syringes, in the air, via machines...they are life-saving and life-threatening, and we were at their mercy. Steroids, x-ray, antibiotics, anesthetic, medications to paralyze, for reflux, morphine...

Harmful-and-Helpful: As each solution comes with its own set of problems, complications require additional treatments, these bring more complications and so on.

When an IV ruptured a vein after a few days or hours, they tried another. They shaved more of her head to find veins until she had only a small patch of hair left in the back.

WHAT WILL SHE DO WHEN SHE'S 14, NOW THAT SHE'S ALREADY HAD A PUNK HAIRSTYLE?

At one point they tried to put in an IV and no more veins would take. They stuck her 18 times and then gave up. They gave her a shot instead.

What are the hip kids in the SCN calling themselves these days?   generation X-tubation.

Why did the chicken cross the road?

to get extubated.

Did you hear about the big spill on the pump room floor?

It was a really big let down.

Did you hear about the preterm baby that enlisted in the army?

He lied about his gestational age.

The list went on. I read them to my mom at Asa's bedside and she nearly wet herself.

Family and friends reached out and were generous.

Some came to visit,

Brought food for us.

From farther away

They sent cards

And gifts for Asa,

Made phone calls,

Sent prayers,

Donated money.

I even got a few massages from my former co-workers at the clinic.

All these helped carry us.

My dad arrived from California and my mom took him to Room 41. Cito was at school and I was eating or pumping. When he saw Asa, he felt so unstable that he lay down on that filthy floor with his head under the crib. The nurses stepped over him until they finally told him to leave.

Later when he came to see me I was busy with something and asked him to heat up some tea. I had the tea in a metal pot and he was so flustered he put the pot in the microwave and the plastic handle shattered.

He stayed for two weeks. He sang songs to Asa and helped out here and there. Our projected time in the hospital lengthened.

Cito and I didn't have a car. My mom had been using a rental car to do all the errands and for her transportation. But a long-term rental was expensive, and my dad decided to buy us a car. I was both ashamed and extremely grateful.

Cito and I had planned to move back to the States in the coming summer. One morning when he and I were both with Asa, Dr. Strideforth came by to check on Asa's progress. After talking with her, we gathered that we could expect a medically unpredictable and possibly complicated year for Asa. At that time there was no guarantee of health insurance in the States.

On a day in the last month of my pregnancy I sat down with the calendar and covered the month with my work schedule, various appointments and to-do lists. Looking at it I had the urgent sense that my next job was to erase nearly everything I'd written down. At the time, I thought this message meant to cancel the plans up to the birth; now I understood it was all the plans from that point on. The future suddenly stood wide open.

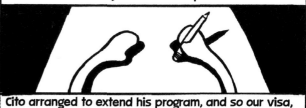

Cito arranged to extend his program, and so our visa, for another year.

Tune told me a funny thing. She normally slept well, but a couple of times she woke up thinking about Asa, or she woke in the morning thinking of her. When this happened she talked to her and sent good thoughts.

A very similar thing happened to Share. She talked about Asa with her two daughters and also her mom. They thought about Asa, meditated on her healing and sent their love. Share's mom had never even met us, but she would call Share and ask, "How's our baby?"

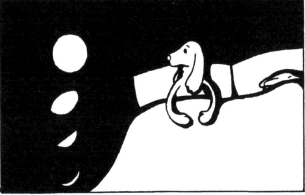

My friend Leaf also woke thinking of Asa. She said prayers for her and sang songs.

Hands was a physiotherapist that began to visit Asa in Room 41. She did massage-like exercises with Asa to help move the phlegm out of her lungs. We liked her and Asa seemed to enjoy the massage. One day Hands told me how she too had woken up thinking of Asa.

I got the feeling that Asa was going out into the night, into the ethers, and rallying her own support.

Despite all the obstacles, Asa was developing normally. After a few weeks she could bring her hands together, and she could focus for long periods of time, tracking moving objects with her eyes or looking at things we showed her. Everyone commented on her bright, alert eyes. At around six weeks she started to smile.

Cito's dad and sister Shell came out from Philadelphia.

Shell asked me how I liked being a mother, and I said I thought I'd love it when we no longer had to work around so much machinery.

Cito's dad took turns holding Asa in our relays, and he stayed for the third trial extubation after the Aortopexy.

It wasn't working. Asa was struggling for air. I was right with her and I could see her ribs heaving in and out. Finally they told me to stand back. This was the first reintubation Cito and I actually saw.

Asa's oxygen levels dropped and kept dropping, with the loud blip on the monitor of her heart rate going slower and slower like she was going to flatline. The charge nurse was standing there with us and saying, "This looks really bad, but it's normal for an intubation. They are taking care of it."

But this was Asa's sixth failed extubation. We'd been at the hospital for over two months and we were back to square one. Asa had taken another beating and the mirage of the way out evaporated. There came the wrecking ball again.

On the last day of my father-in-law's visit, he was holding Asa and I was out pumping. Cito was at school and my mom was in and out of 41. When I came back in and looked at Asa, her face was very red, in fact there was almost a purple tinge.

And suddenly she did start to turn purple and then she started to turn blue. The ET tube had slipped; this was an accidental extubation.

I could see the terror in her eyes. I looked at the screen and saw her SATs. The line was plummeting down and the number was already down near 60. I called out to N. Sure.

SHE'S TURNING BLUE!

GET AN R.T STAT!

She was saying the tube had come out. I was panicking, saying, "She can't breathe without the tube!" But in order to reintubate it has to come out. They can't just shove it in a little further.

It seemed like ages before the doctors and the RTs arrived, but suddenly there was a crowd around Asa's bed and they were trying to reintubate her. I was standing back and my mom had come in. I was talking to myself, like "It's okay, they're reintubating, they're handling it. It's okay."

But I could see they were having difficulty. I kept looking at the screen to see her SATs. They were extremely low. As was her heartbeat.

My mom came over and I shook her off. I didn't want her touching me, there was nothing she could do to comfort me at that moment.

I could see one of the RTs was listening to see if the tube was in the right place, and she said, "It's in her stomach." It had gone down the wrong way. I looked at the RT. She pulled the stethoscope away from her ears and shook her head in this dire way.

There was a nurse who was with a couple of babies from the other side of the room. She was nearby and watching. I went over to her and said, "Tell me what's going on."

I wanted her to help me understand and tell me it was okay, the way the charge nurse from before had narrated the intubation for Cito and me. She just looked at me and didn't answer, maybe because I was starting to lose it.

I said again, "Tell me what's going on." I looked at her and saw she was crying. And that's when I thought Asa was dying.

It was as if the whole room were collapsing on me. We'd come all this way and been through so much, and now Asa was dying right before my eyes. And I stumbled off to the side of the room, and started to go down to the floor.

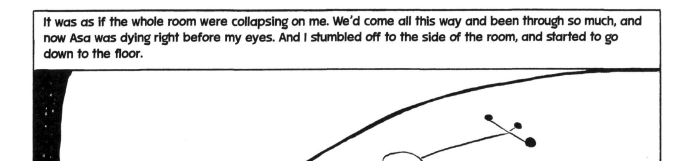

The next thing I knew my mom and Cito's dad were over with me saying, "Here, sit in this chair, sit in this chair." And I sat down and they were saying, "Asa's okay, they got her intubated and she's okay."

It took me a while to come back to real time, to where they said, "She's okay, she's alive."

Another nurse had come over and was going on about hospital policy: That they reintubated Asa because that was hospital policy.
And they weren't going to let anything happen to her because it was hospital policy. And I was like: Policy?!

I wanted to know if Asa had brain damage. They said no, her oxygen deprivation didn't go on that long. I asked if they were sure and they said yes.

Asa had a dazed look on her face, which was puffy from the emergency maneuvers and medications. She looked like a little kitten. She was alive.

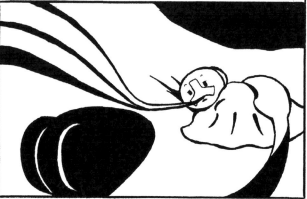

We were lucky that N. Sure had the shift with Asa that day. She had almost 20 years of experience in the unit, and her calm direction of the intubation likely saved Asa's life.

Cito arrived shortly after it was all over. He and I went out to talk, and his dad stayed with Asa, who was now asleep. I'd thought Asa was dying. After this I started having a harder time pulling myself together.

The next morning during the doctor's rounds Cito, my mom and I were with Asa. They went over what had happened the night before and asked if we had any questions. I got up from my chair and said, "We no longer feel Asa is safe on the ventilator. What happened yesterday could happen at any time. She's just getting bigger and stronger so it's harder to keep her intubated."

We didn't know much about tracheostomy, but we knew she could leave the hospital with one. We knew we could pick her up and hold her, and that she could start to learn to eat orally. I said, "If that's what we need to do, then that's what we need to do. But she's no longer safe on the ventilator and that's clear."

The doctor who had rotated into being in charge of her case was Dr. Eyes. He stepped forward and said, "Yes, I agree completely. It's time to go to the next step."

Dr. Eyes organized a meeting for everyone who was directly concerned. Dr. Littlebox came with his residents, and Dr. Storytime from transitional care was there, whom Dr. Littlebox called "The Trake Man." Dr. Eyes said, "You have to know it's not like she gets the trake and then you go home. She has to recover and you have to do your training, how to take care of her, and that training takes from four to six weeks. You're looking at being in the hospital another six to eight weeks at least."

Things were getting blurry for me and the notion of when we might leave the hospital was a vague horizon. Sometimes back at night I asked Cito if he thought we really would get to take Asa home someday and he said,

I KNOW WE WILL.

The surgery was a few days later. Cito and I told her what was happening, that she was safe and surrounded by love and light, that this was important to help her breathe and it was a step toward going home. We said, "You are protected and in good hands." We walked down the hall and she went in. And we waited.

Dr. Littlebox had made his first estimate that Asa might have the trake for two to four months. But by now they realized the Tracheomalacia was quite severe. He said her trachea needed time to grow bigger and develop more cartilage.

SIX TO EIGHTEEN MONTHS, EH?

Back in the NICU they had Asa paralyzed for 48 hours, looking somewhere between asleep and dead. The trake was in her neck and the ventilator hooked up to that, and there were two sutures with long black threads hanging down her chest. These were to help open her airway in case the trake became dislodged before the stoma (the surgically-made hole) could heal.

There was a tube coming out of her neck, my baby's sweet, perfect neck, an aberration. But we were dependent on it.

It was our bridge.

That night I made my way back to the Haunter House feeling we had crossed an irreversible line. The air around me was as vacuous and desolate as after her birth. My innocent one, my little cub. How dare this happen to her.

Floating in the barbaric limbo of post-op. It's a grinding, eternal twilight. Heart rate, blood pressure, medication, respiration.

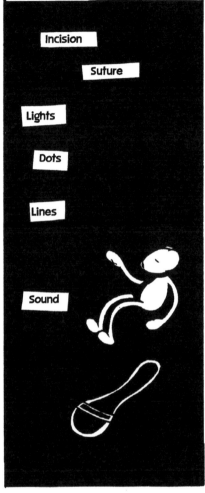

I went through the security doors and down the hall. Web stepped out of the office as I passed. "How are you?" She put her arm around my shoulders. She'd worked as a nurse for years and kept up on Asa's progress.

"She got traked today," I said. I could barely feel the ground beneath my feet, but her kind arm was steady and it helped a bit.

Chuckles was on in the first critical days. He took such good care of her. He showed us how we could tell by her heart rate if she was asleep, awake, in pain, and explained that she could hear us. Her heart rate went down when she heard our voices, and her SATs went up. Chuckles showed me how to do gentle range-of-motion exercises with her while she was still paralyzed.
He was our hero.

When Asa was off the paralyzing drug and the morphine was lower, they took her off the ventilator. The trake held her airway open. It was about seven days before we could hold her again. But then we could pick her up ourselves. Pick her up out of the bed and hold her. Imagine, we could pick her up and see most of her face.

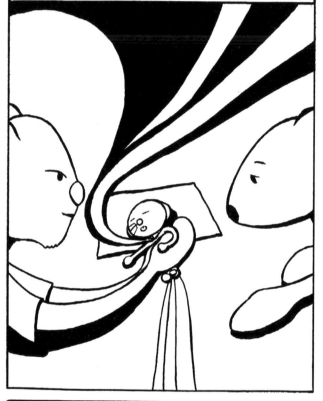

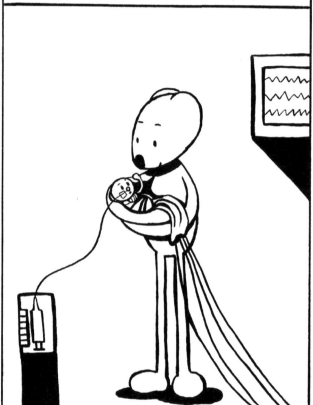

Concerns, the occupational therapist, came to assess her swallow and thought we could begin to work on oral feeding.

With the advice of a lactation consultant we started trying the breast. Asa had a good rooting reflex but she had a hard time latching on. She got frustrated from trying. She shook her head back and forth faster and faster and then would cry.

After about a week I decided we should focus on the bottle, since the nipple was more like her soother. I wanted her to breastfeed, but eating orally via whatever method was more important.

The South

In a section of the NICU called "The South" there were several isolation rooms. Usually these rooms were for babies with dangerous infections, but now there was an empty room and we asked if Asa could stay there. This way she would be away from the noise and glare of 41. She could have some relative quiet and also relative dark at night. So we left 41 and relocated her.
The isolation room was quieter, but there was no nurse present like there was in 41.

Asa was still being fed round the clock and vomiting accordingly. As with the ET, because of the trake, she needed constant suctioning. Suctioning sometimes made her throw up, but then so did coughing.

Now she had an open hole straight into her lungs. I was terrified she would puke into her trake in the night and die. If she choked, de-SAT-ing would of course set off the alarm on the monitor, but alarms in the unit seemed always to be ringing without anyone checking on them.

Cito started staying up later into the night, and I got up earlier. When I woke up to pump or couldn't sleep I called the nurses' station to check on her.

Once when I arrived in the morning, Asa was awake and crying. There was no way to know how long she'd been crying since her cry was only slightly louder than her breathing. With the trake, no air passed through the vocal cords, so we still couldn't hear her voice. But now she made a noise, "Khh Khh" because of the mucus in the tube.

Dr. Net, my chiropractor, and his wife visited us twice in this room.

I held Asa while Dr. Net worked his light touch on her spine, which allowed her nervous system to unwind from trauma.

A week or two later we were able to move into a different isolation room, one with a window, and Asa could look outside for the first time.

Asa had been on morphine every day of her life because of all the surgeries.

High doses of morphine have to be reduced slowly, and there was never enough time between surgeries and procedures to come off it completely. And the longer a person is on it, the slower it has to be reduced.

Asa's dose was reduced in small increments every couple of days, but even so she began to have withdrawal symptoms.

She became agitated and jumpy. She startled at nothing and flung her limbs.

She sneezed, had explosive green diarrhea, and cried endlessly.

It went on for weeks.

She seemed so miserable. It was getting harder for me to resurface during this period. I began thinking we had made a dreadful mistake, or I had made a dreadful mistake, bringing a baby into the world only to suffer, and these thoughts hammered at me during my sleepless nights.

One night, my mom stopped by the Haunter House to get herself some dinner before going home. I was sitting on the bed and she was about to leave, and I let fall a few tears.

She had said recently that she wanted to help with more than just food and laundry, she wanted to be an emotional support too. Now I thought maybe, just this once, she could tell me that things would turn out okay. Instead she offered up a lecture on the way I was mishandling myself.

I said I couldn't talk to her if she couldn't be 'open-hearted,' using one of her favorite phrases.

It was similar to times long in the past when she'd wanted me to share my feelings. But when I dared, it was a complete fiasco.

She thought I ought to "do something," by which she meant get on medication.

I thought it was natural for a person in my position to be upset.

Then again, maybe she saw something I didn't.

I was holding Asa, watching her sleep and listening to her breathe through the mucus. My mom came in and sat down in an extra rocking chair. She'd been reading a book on infant development.

Infants are distressed when confronted with "stone face," a cold and unresponsive expression on the mother's face. She said, "I think that's what I received."

I was stunned. Actually I knew about stone face, if you wanted to call it that. I saw it on her on a regular basis when I was a kid, though this wasn't part of her revelation.

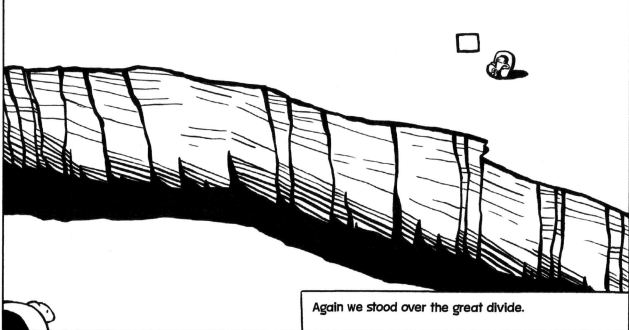

Again we stood over the great divide.

By April the trees were flowering and it was spring. Enclosed in the hospital it was like watching the seasons change on TV, through the occasional sealed window.

Once in a while I took walks and picked flowers to put in the room at Haunter House. I tried to be outside for both Asa and myself. I told her so as I walked, in my mind or out loud. "These are things you'll get to see one day."

We couldn't bring flowers into the unit, but we decorated Asa's crib with pictures and hanging toys.

Sometimes we propped open a book for her to look at.

HOW IS SHE?

SHE'S WATCHING T.V.

We started oral feeding by trying the bottle about half an hour before the tube feedings. We had these tiny bottles and red nipples that didn't require a strong suck. She took ten ml, then 20, then 30. We had heard from another parent in the NICU whose daughter was traked a month before Asa, that the doctor told them they could go home when she could take half her food by mouth. Asa was getting about 90 ml of breast milk every three hours, so we weren't far from that if Asa would take the bottle at every feed.

Then Asa started to refuse the bottle. With the help of Concerns, the OT, we tried some other kinds of nipples. Asa had missed the window for instinctive oral feeding, and after having all kinds of things shoved in her mouth, the bottle feeding was a sensitive issue. You can't force a baby to suck, especially a crying baby, and by trying you can make her more adverse. Everyone said keep trying. But we were backsliding.

One of the lactation consultants had told me earlier not to be frustrated if oral feeding didn't take off right away. I told her after all the airway issues, the feeding would be no big deal, but I was wrong. I began to dread getting out the bottle. If oral feeding didn't progress, the recommendation was to have a feeding tube put surgically directly into her stomach. The last thing we wanted was another surgery.

We bought Asa some infant acidophilus to put in the milk, to build her intestinal flora after so many rounds of antibiotics.

Once my mom was trying to feed Asa and she was refusing the bottle. Sometimes her way of refusing was to fall asleep so deeply it was impossible to wake her.

My mom wondered if the acidophilus made the milk taste different, and to test her theory tipped up the bottle and shook a few drops into her mouth.

Chuckles was on with Asa that day and just then walked in.

WHAT ARE YOU DOING??

UH, I GUESS IF IT'S YOUR DAUGHTER'S IT'S OKAY...

NO. NO, IT'S NOT OKAY!

Later she tried to explain.

Cito and I met with N. Kindskill and RT Bat from transitional care to arrange our trake training.

This would be twice a week for three hours at a time. My mom took the training too, and some friends stayed with Asa during the sessions.

Each time, Bat met us in the South with her cart of trake supplies, including a plastic baby doll, much like the doll from my dreams.

Asa would need to be on a humidifier at night. This meant having sterile water to put in the humidifier, two liters per night, plus masks and tubing. For suctioning she needed two suction machines, manual suction devices in case these failed, about 200 catheters per month, 60 bottles of saline, boxes of single-use sterile saline, gauze, drying powder, tubing and string for her trake ties, lubricant and extra trakes for emergency trake changes, a resuscitation bag should she stop breathing, silver nitrate for granulomas, boxes of filters that covered the trake, also known as humidivents, AKA heat and moisture exchangers, AKA Swedish noses. She needed an oximeter (a monitor for her heart rate and oxygen saturation), boxes of SAT probes to tape to her foot at night, syringes, cases of vinegar for cleaning equipment, and boxes of gloves. There was a long list of supplies for tube feeding as well, depending on how the oral feeding went.

As a Canadian citizen, Asa qualified for a program that covered all her supply expenses and delivered them every two months. We were fortunate to be in Canada, as would continue to dawn on us. In the States, we would have been up the proverbial creek.

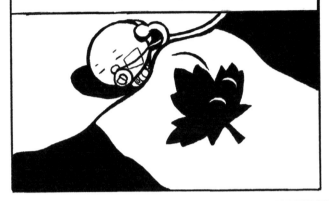

The program might also provide respite nursing care. This was especially critical since someone had to be awake with Asa all night. She needed suctioning and feeding during the night. At any moment she could cough up a blob of mucus thick enough to plug the trake completely. And of course there was the vomiting. She would be on the monitor but that was a machine that could fail. Bat reminded us of this and so did Dr. Storytime.

Our apartment was tiny, a kitchen, a bedroom, and a bathroom we shared with two other people. We had no room to store all the equipment, no space to change Asa's trake ties, and no way to accommodate a nurse during the night. It became clear we had to move. My mom put "find apartment" on her to-do list. Which in Vancouver was like a needle in a haystack.

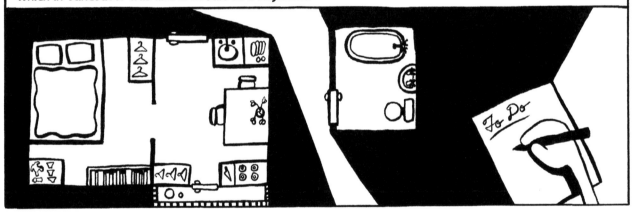

With each session the scope of our situation expanded. Taking in and processing the information was rather like smaller hits from the wrecking ball, because we learned how vulnerable Asa was and how complicated and constant her care.

We'd thought the worst was behind us and now I wasn't sure. Cito was frustrated with my downcast attitude. He reminded me, "This is the situation we're in, we have to accept it, rise to the occasion." I promised to try and take the bull by the horns.

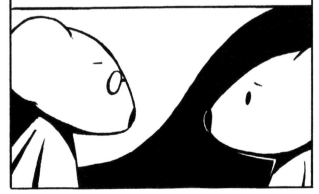

We learned how and when to suction, how to use saline to clear dry, plug-forming mucus, how to use the "noses." We learned how to change the ties that held the trake in place, a precarious choreography during which the trake could accidentally come out.

We learned to change the trake tube itself, and how to handle a number of emergency situations. Because of the trake, Asa was also at risk for chest infections, pneumonia, and problems with tooth enamel. She could have problems with hearing, balance, movement, could need other procedures, or surgeries.

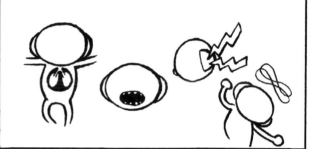

Using the portable Suction Machine

OKAY, LET'S SAY YOU'RE AT THE MALL

WRONG!

OKAY, LET'S SAY YOU'RE AT THE PARK...

CLIK!

RRR RRR

SHIT!

Once we had learned something with Bat, we started practicing it under the supervision of the nurses and RTs. So we began to do the suctioning, and the assessment of Asa's breathing. Would the secretions or a suction be more likely to cause her to throw up? She had to keep down enough food to be healthy and grow, for her organs and brain to develop properly. Everything had hefty consequences.

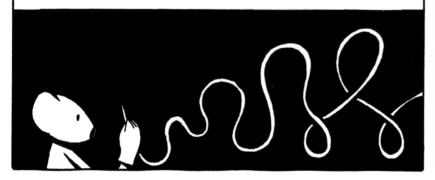

At night I called the room in the South. Cito put Asa up to the receiver. I could hear her breathing and talk to her.

KHHH KHHH KHAA

I LOVE YOU SWEETPEA.

Cito was very proactive about the training. He wanted to know everything involved in Asa's care right away, things they weren't even teaching us. He had the nurses show him how to draw up Asa's medications into syringes...

And give them to her in the NG tube, and how to work the feeding pump.

He said, "Asa is so fabulous."

When we went between Asa's room and the Haunter House the route took us down behind the cafeteria and through the more industrial workings of the hospital laundry and beyond. Late at night or early in the morning you rarely saw another person. Cito said he wished he had a go-cart he could drive along these long, deserted corridors.

I kept losing my way in the dark, and he hung on to the light.

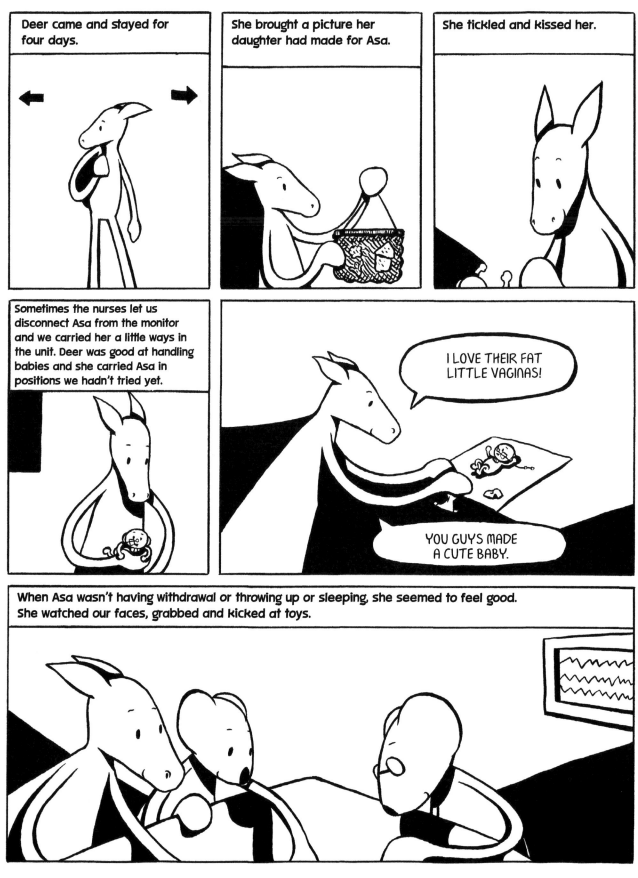

Deer came and stayed for four days.

She brought a picture her daughter had made for Asa.

She tickled and kissed her.

Sometimes the nurses let us disconnect Asa from the monitor and we carried her a little ways in the unit. Deer was good at handling babies and she carried Asa in positions we hadn't tried yet.

I LOVE THEIR FAT LITTLE VAGINAS!

YOU GUYS MADE A CUTE BABY.

When Asa wasn't having withdrawal or throwing up or sleeping, she seemed to feel good. She watched our faces, grabbed and kicked at toys.

Cito and I had to decide whether to give Asa any vaccines. Vaccines were routine at the hospital, and lots of them. I'd said I didn't want her to have any, since reading that I'd done connected them with brain and nervous system injury that let to autism and other diseases, brain damage and even death. The doctors were considerate, but pushed the vaccines. There were infectious diseases that could lead to brain damage and death as well, and Asa was especially vulnerable to certain illnesses because of the trake.

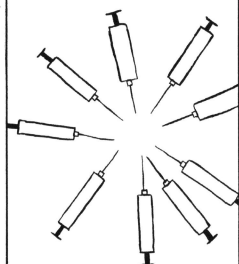

Cito and I did as much research as we could. It was easy to find information both for and against. It was a roulette of risk. Cito was for and I was against.

During this time, a baby across the corridor, who had been born healthy, died of some kind of infection. I was with Asa and Deer and Concerns talking about Asa's feeding when alarms went off. Doctors and nurses rushed in and then we heard the mother sobbing. I felt her very near to me. This was one of the things that convinced Cito we should go for the vaccine.

Deer and I took a walk in a park near the hospital. We sat near the duck pond. Trees swayed, families with tubeless kids wandered by.

Earlier that day, I'd asked the advice of a family friend who regularly visited the unknown. She heard Asa say, "Protect my lungs." And she suggested using all available tools.

Maybe it seems minor, a drop in the bucket. But to decide for vaccine meant opening my mind with a crowbar. I told Cito I would agree to one shot. This was a five-in-one that included whooping cough, with no mercury. I said, "One shot. We'll decide on the next move after we see how that goes."

To prepare for the shot we asked the doctors to pause in lowering the morphine dosage, to keep it steady for several days. This way Asa's body wouldn't have to deal with the withdrawal and the vaccine at the same time. Afterwards, she cried and then calmed down.

I told Asa she was a big strong tree. that she had big strong roots going into the ground connecting her to the earth. Those roots pulled in the earth energy to nourish and support her. She could weather any storm, and had big strong branches that reached into the sky and pulled in the light. I could see the tree full of peace and strength. Cito said listening to this meditation made him feel better too. He stayed in the room with Asa all that night.

Cito and I took over bathing Asa, which needed to be done before the trake-tie change, and in the small window between feeds and pumping. All day was a rush.

Cito and I did the trake ties for the first time by ourselves. It took all our concentration since we had to work together in the right steps and keep the trake in place. We cut the ties, cleaned her neck and under the trake flanges and put on a new tie. I'd slept three hours the night before and my hands were shaking.

Later Cito and I went to look at the potential apartment Deer and my mom had found by driving around our neighborhood, and to meet the owners who lived upstairs. This was the second time I had left the hospital.

Our neighborhood seemed like heaven. Trees, dogs...but you can't enjoy your visit to heaven too much with your baby still in hell.

The apartment and the people were nice. We tried not to appear desperate. Chatting was like the biggest charade of my life.

We gave them some references and a few days later they called to say we could rent the place when it was ready.

It was Mother's Day. I raced to the nursery in the early morning as usual. The room was decorated.

The night before Cito had put up pictures and little pretend notes from Asa. It was the first time I smiled in a long time.

He came down to the room later, and so did Deer and my mom. My mom took pictures of the three of us holding Asa, and of the decorated room.

One morning while Cito and I were hurriedly trying to do Asa's bath and trake ties, a woman came by to introduce herself. She was Dr. Pert, the staff psychologist from transitional care. She said to give her a call if we needed anything. I was pretty flustered and she left after a minute.

Outwardly, things were improving but I felt I was doing poorly. I started having spaces of time where I didn't feel in my right mind. I did my best to keep it together when I was with Asa, but then I would go back to the Haunter House and fall apart. I was alone with my fears and getting more and more nervous.

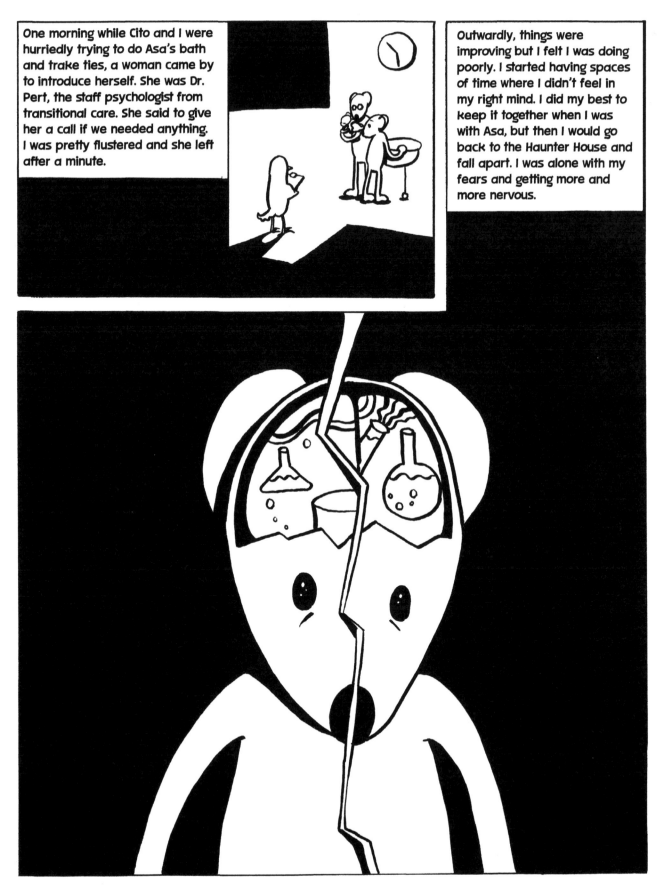

One day one of the RTs found a growth of granulation tissue on the stoma of Asa's trake. It needed to be burned off in a series of treatments using silver nitrate. Even though they said it wasn't a big deal, I was wrecked. All I could think was: More toxins, more procedures.

Each night I went to the kitchen to get something for dinner and make a lunch for the next day. Making a sandwich seemed like a calculus problem. I'd be standing there at the counter with a knife and pieces of bread, panicking.

All day I was naked under lights in a world of strangers. At night alone in the dark with no air. It had been 103 days and 104 nights.

The night before Deer left, I called her and my mom from the Haunter House. I was worried about my mental health. I spoke to my mom, I said I was afraid I could wind up in the hospital myself. She said, "Let's not be dramatic."

But after Deer left, my grip slipped more.

The discharge nurse coordinated a meeting for those involved to plan out the rest of Asa's time in the hospital. We met in the tiny conference room where we'd discussed Asa's tracheostomy. Dr. Storytime was there again, one or two of the doctors from the NICU, a community health nurse who would be presenting Asa's case to the ministry for nursing support, Bat, and N. Kindskill facilitating.

I was on a loveseat, wedged between Cito and my mom. They listed the steps leading to Asa's discharge including: the completion of our training, the question of another surgery for the gastrostomy tube, and the care-by-parent weekend—when Cito and I would take care of Asa alone for 48 hours in another part of the hospital. They set a tentative date for the middle of June.

The case was my daughter, my life. It had become so alien. I had an overwhelming desire to sleep. The room was full of people who could not have been more dedicated, more skilled, all assembled for the sole purpose of helping us. And I loathed them, every single one.

I couldn't imagine how we would ever handle taking care of Asa once we left the hospital. I couldn't imagine even leaving the hospital. I couldn't imagine staying in the hospital. I was stuck on: How did this ever happen? How did we ever get here?

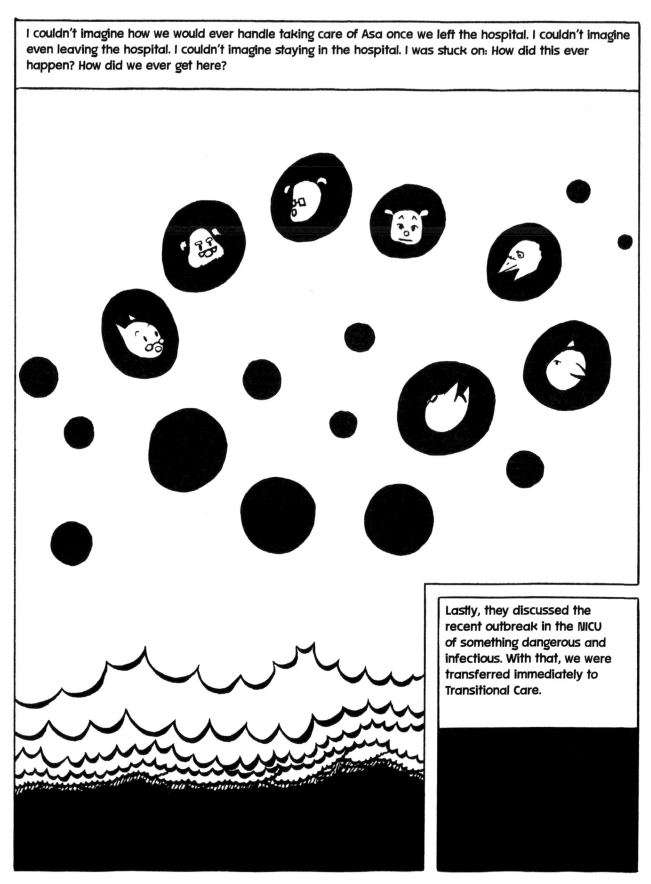

Lastly, they discussed the recent outbreak in the NICU of something dangerous and infectious. With that, we were transferred immediately to Transitional Care.

The TCU

The Transitional Care Unit was a section of the children's intensive care. It turned out to be the most dreadful place I'd ever been. Dark, with searing fluorescent spotlights, cold and full of dying and broken children, frozen inside various contraptions, casts, ventilators, and all exposed to the entire unit.

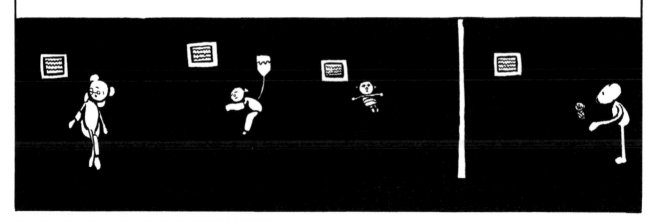

Stricken parents and families staggered in the hallways or leaned against walls, bald kids from oncology walked or wheeled by with the IV pumps from their chemotherapy. It seemed like Armageddon. Asa lived there now, so we did too.

I ate lunch in the NICU parent lounge because there was a refrigerator, it was near the pump room, and because it was less horrible.

Though one day a nurse ran in saying that she needed some juice from the fridge, and I said I didn't know what belonged to whom.

She ran out again with a cup of juice. A few meters away, another child was dying in front of its mother.

I had more and longer periods when nothing seemed quite real, and it became harder to function.

A crushing despair weighed relentlessly over all the minutes and hours of the clock.

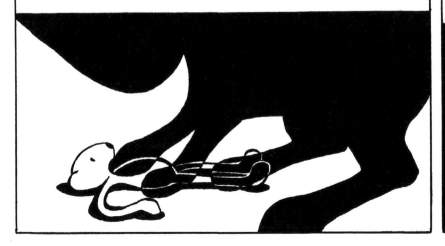

I wondered what it would be like to take all the sleeping pills in the little jar by my bed.

At the bottom of this pit, along with the paramount of my fears, that Asa would die, was the thought that her death might set me free.

Then I knew I was truly a monster.

Dr. Pert, the TCU psychologist, came by one day when I was with Asa. I asked if we could meet and she turned out to be a good person to talk to. I started seeing her once a week. In her office I rambled, incoherently I thought, but she said,

I FOLLOW YOU.

Every morning I scraped myself out of bed, to the pump, and ran down to the unit. I chanted to myself "Everything is fine and I feel great," over and over.

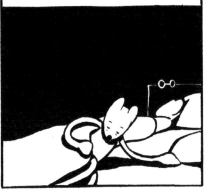

The morning was a confusion of suctioning, diapers, feeding, crying, vomiting, bottle rejecting, near choking, coughing, etc. Often Asa vomited and needed immediate suctioning when I was in the middle of a diaper change. It was impossible for only two hands to cover everything. I'd ring for the nurse and wonder how this would be remotely possible at home.

But there were also periods of calm when Asa slept or was awake, watchful, playful and smiling.

One morning I saw another mother changing her baby's diaper. She was leaning over the baby and smiling sweetly. By then, I could barely force a smile for Asa. I was nothing like this other woman, I thought.

This mother had twins, one with a trake, who was in the unit for a surgery to remove granulation tissue that had formed in her trachea. They'd been home from the hospital for two months. "I went to suction and I got blood. I called 911," she said. We'd learned to do the same in our training.

Later I asked Bat about internal granulomas with trakes and if it could happen to Asa. She said it could. I asked what were the chances, but she just said,

IT COULD HAPPEN.

Not long after this there was a small amount of blood in Asa's secretions, and a scope showed an internal granuloma.

Right around this time I had been using the practice trake from Bat's cart to see if my measurement of the suction catheter was different when I had gloves on versus when I didn't.

Because the length of the trake tube was 5.5 centimeters, we grasped the catheter at the 6 cm mark. This allowed the end of the catheter to pass a few millimeters out the end of the trake tube. Going farther than this would damage the trachea and less might be ineffective for suctioning.

.5cm

With the practice trake I noticed the suction catheter when grasped at 6 cm passed nearly a full centimeter outside of the trake tube. These few millimeters could be a life and death difference. Bat said the measurements must have been off.

After that we always suctioned at 5.5 cm and the blood in the secretions disappeared.
Dr. Storytime said we would wait a few weeks and do another scope.

It was evening and I was in the communal kitchen with my mom. She was washing dishes and I was trying to do the impossible: Put some food from a large container into a small one for my lunch the next day.

I went back to my room to get something and when I returned to the kitchen, my mom had put the food back into the large container. I stared at it, feeling panic rush in. I tried to get words out of my mouth.

JUST LET IT GO! LET IT GO!

I lost it.

ARRRGH!!!

CALM DOWN!

GET AWAY FROM ME!

I thought I could be violent.

I got myself into a corner to try to be away from her.

MY HEART IS OPEN! MY HEART IS...

I DON'T CARE!!

I pulled a sweatshirt that was next to me and screamed into it like an animal.

PLEASE DON'T DO THIS...

PLEASE DON'T DO THIS...

While one part of me felt out of control, another part wondered why, being a psychotherapist, my mom didn't know how to handle someone flipping out. And another part of me felt bad for her: With her granddaughter in intensive care and her daughter losing her mind.

DON'T DO THIS.

WHY? BECAUSE THEY'LL COME AND SEDATE ME?

MAYBE.

She left to go talk to Web in the office, to tell her everything was okay. And then she went down to the unit to be with Asa, so Cito could come up and stay with me.

Two days later, when we were both in the TCU with Asa, my mom asked me, "What need were you attempting to meet by screaming?" I answered that I was a primate in distress. I couldn't fathom her question and she wasn't satisfied with my answer.

After this, it was clear I had to get my shit together. Asa deserved better, so did Cito, so even did I. And even my mom. I spoke with Deer on the phone. A friend of hers didn't like the term "depression" but instead preferred "Horror-Brain." We've all got a horror-brain, and given the right inputs, one can get stuck there. I could relate to this; I needed all the help I could get getting unstuck. I never thought I would go on antidepressants, but I decided to try it.

I saw the psychiatrist that had prescribed the sleeping pills. She gave me Equil, which was supposed to be relatively safe for breast milk.

I called Bloom, a peer counseling teacher. He told me I should be talking to someone every day. I got the phone numbers of three family friends and asked them if I could call them for help. So sometimes in the evenings I called Deer, or Bloom, or one of the three friends. I asked them to help me think positively, or help me calm down.

I started to take a walk outside every day. I walked quickly and sought out the hills to try to get my heart beating faster and some endorphins flowing.

A few times I walked over to the park I'd been to with Deer. One time a couple lounging in the grass flagged me down. They were on holiday from Argentina and wanted me to take their picture. They asked me if I was from nearby and I told them my daughter was a patient at the hospital.

At once they asked me if I wanted them to say a prayer for her. I wanted all the prayers I could get for Asa, and anyway Jesus was Jewish, so why not? They were very earnest and called for God and his son to heal Asa. And I thanked them for it.

One of the nurses that tended to me in the aftermath of Asa's birth came back from her break and said, "I said a prayer for your little girl." I guessed that that one went out to Allah, and together with the other prayers from family and friends, I thought we had a good number of the world's major and minor deities covered.

One day when Cito was with Asa, my mom and I took a long walk at the park. It was part of a plan to be less isolated with my horror brain.

She bought me a new pair of sunglasses on the way.

She told me the story of a blind man and a deaf man who drove across the country to adopt a blind and deaf dog.

She oohed and aahed over flowers.

She laughed at a little dog that did circus tricks.

I wanted to lie down a little on the top of a hill and she laid down her jacket for me.

She was there, she'd stuck it out all this time. She was doing her best and she cared about me. And we made a little bit of peace there.

One part of our training was to do a "trake change." This was a procedure where we removed the trake tube and put in a new one. It had to be done quickly since Asa couldn't breathe until the new one was in. Bat helped Cito do his first trake change. Dr. Storytime and N. Terrafirma, were standing by in case anything went wrong, and my mom and I were watching. He did it perfectly and I was so proud of him. I thought he was so brave.

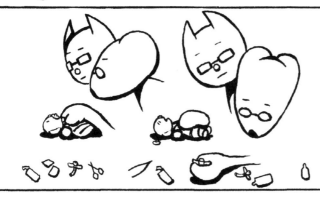

Once one of us had done the trake change we were allowed to unhook Asa from the monitor and take her outside the unit with a portable suction machine. The first time we took her just a little way down the corridor, and the second time we took her outside to a small courtyard. It was cold and we had her bundled up. We showed her a bush. We showed her a tree. The sky. "Look!" I kept saying, "Nature!"

I did my first trake change a few weeks later. I removed the plastic tube from the hole in the soft flesh of Asa's neck, and put in a new one.

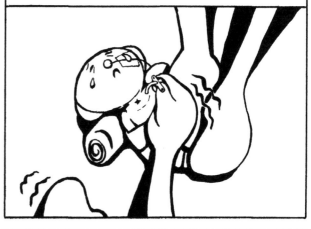

Asa could now go outside the hospital, or travel within the corridors with us, to lounges or the Haunter House. Eventually we went as far as a block or two away: To a small park my mom called "toilet park" in honor of the less-than-fresh bathroom.

This was a lot to manage: The loads of supplies for suctioning, emergency trake changes and supplies for feeding; saline and noses, gloves and catheters, clean or sterile, and Asa's breathing had to be checked at every moment. But Asa was seeing new things, at least.

I could hold Asa on my lap, and she could look at the sun and shadows swaying and reach out her hands to catch them.

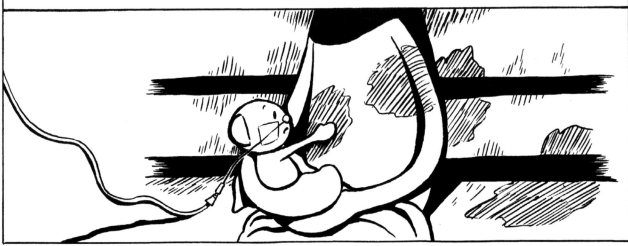

A family we'd heard about in the NICU were admitted to the TCU. Baby M. was about a year older than Asa and had a trake. She was in for surgery that would hopefully allow her to breathe without it.

YOU DO GET USED TO THE TRAKE, EH? IT BECOMES NORMAL.

COUGH COUGH COUGH COUGH BARF

OH FOR ALL THE STUFF, EH?

IS THIS THE KIND OF STROLLER WE SHOULD GET?

RIGHT.

WE PUT THE SUCTION MACHINE HERE, YOU THROW YOUR OXYGEN DOWN THERE...

LUCKILY WE DON'T NEED OXYGEN.

PERFECT!

WAIT! DON'T MOVE HER! SHE'LL LOSE THE REST OF HER FEED!

WELL WE CAN'T HAVE HER SITTING IN VOMIT.

Baby M. was on a ventilator during her post-op and kept trying to pull out the tube, which we knew was highly dangerous.

IT'S NERVE-WRACKING. BUT SHE'S A FIGHTER AND I'M GLAD SHE'S A FIGHTER.

WELL IT DOESN'T HURT TO BE POSITIVE.

They had been waiting a year for that operation and in the end Baby M. still needed the trake.

THIS IS HOW WE KNOW HOW TO BE PARENTS.

SO WE'LL JUST KEEP GOING.

Their attitude was incredible.

My mom brought in a toy spider. It had a bell inside the body and a different kind of cloth shoe on each foot with rattles and crinkly paper inside them. Asa got a look of excited concentration and tried to bat at all the parts. She loved it. We kept it next to her in the bed.

One early morning I rushed to the TCU hoping Asa would still be asleep. But she was awake, lying there all alone, tiny girl in her dark cavern.

She had ahold of one of the spider's legs and was pulling it just a little, back and forth.

Asa's feeding still wasn't progressing and they had to check her swallow. Without being able to swallow properly a person might never be able to eat by mouth.

OKAY, GIVE THE BOTTLE ANOTHER SQUEEZE.

DOING GREAT SWEETPEA.

In radiology, they put me in a lead apron and put us both between big sheets of clanging metal. I gave her a bottle of barium solution and luckily she took enough that they could make their movie.

Everyone was beaming. She could swallow and protect her airway, though her suck was weak. Concerns showed me the video afterward and pointed out the place where her esophagus had been repaired. Below this, her esophagus didn't have the usual muscle action, which meant she might always need to drink while eating.

Later that afternoon N. Kindskill stopped by the unit to tell us Asa had been approved for 56 hours of respite care per week. Canada had a shortage of nurses, but providing there was enough staff, Asa could have a nurse almost every night.

We had two pieces of good news in one day.

I passed Dr. Storytime in the hall. He said,

IT'S SO NICE TO SEE YOU SMILE!

A few days later N. Cheerful and N. Elegance from nursing support services visited us to explain the ins and outs of nursing care at home.

N. Cheerful explained that once a baby was at home it usually took a few months to get the staff in place. Hopefully they would be able to put a team together for Asa by the end of summer.

In the meantime, they said, N. Cheerful should be able to cover two to four nights a week, as long as no one called in sick in the NICU. She said her fingers were crossed.

It was impossible for me to imagine how Cito and I would handle Asa's care outside of the hospital, especially now that we knew one of us would stay awake all night three to five times a week.

I was holding Asa and I began to fall asleep right in front of them. I apologized for being practically narcoleptic and my mom burst out laughing.

I didn't know how much N. Cheerful's crossed fingers might help, but maybe if I just went to sleep I'd wake up and our stacked-up problems would be solved.

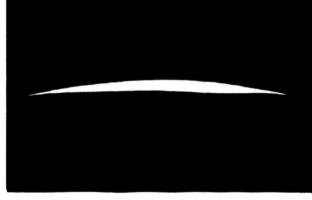

As Asa grew bigger and more dexterous, the feeding tube in her nose became more of a problem. She pulled or coughed it out often. A dislodged tube was hard to put back in, and a partially dislodged tube could put milk straight into her lungs.

The tube was held on by tape that had to be pulled off and re-adhered, which was awful, and Asa was still rejecting the bottle. Concerns said it could take several months, even years, to get her feeding orally. Everyone recommended the Gastrostomy Surgery—the "G-tube"—that would put a feeding tube directly into her stomach. Cito and I agreed.

In Dr. Pert's office, I spoke my fear of more trauma for Asa. Dr. Pert said, "It's going to be a challenge for her, but this is about your trauma, not hers." I thought possibly she had a point, and I tried to readjust my thinking.

Cito and I saw Chuckles in the hall and told him about the surgery. He sighed, but reassured us that kids recover quickly from these, and that it wasn't a major operation.

We did our best to get ourselves and Asa ready. And we got through it.

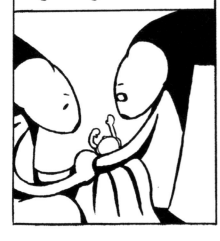

As Asa recovered, we learned to use the G-tube, and to care for the site, and we saw her little face without anything on it.

My mom had been getting supplies for our new place.

She borrowed tools from our landlord and built a bed for Asa.

And then gave him some of the tomatoes and herbs she'd grown on the apartment balcony.

She had an uncanny knack for finding exactly what we needed in alleys and at yard sales.

She even found three Mormon boys to help with the move.

And when the car lost a hub cap, she found a perfect match lying in the street.

In early June, a friend from California and another from Seattle came to help us move.

About two weeks later we had our care-by-parent weekend. With the help of N. Terrafirma, we loaded carts with all of Asa's machines and supplies and traveled to an upper floor of the hospital that had real rooms.

We relocated Asa and worked out the puzzle of where to hook up or stack or wash or dry or stow or cram everything. Besides Asa's bed and other things there was a sink, a small bed, and next to that, a small cabinet.

Weirdly, every few minutes a sound like heavy furniture being dragged echoed through the wall.

When night fell, it was the first time we didn't have to leave Asa, and the first time the three of us were together overnight.
It was a remarkable feeling.

But it was also complicated.

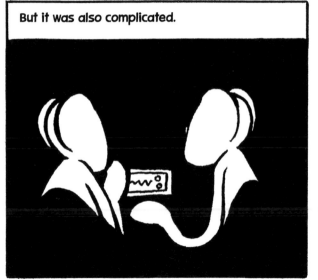

The oxygen and heart-rate monitor we would be using at home malfunctioned, and when we couldn't figure it out we called an RT from downstairs.

In the next 45 hours every moment was consumed with suctioning, tube feeding, pumping (for me of course), checking Asa's breathing and equipment, washing bags, bottles, tubes, syringes and pump parts, changing trake ties, diapers and clothing, and cleaning vomit.

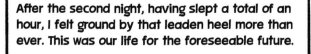

There were a few minutes here and there for a walk down the hall.

After the second night, having slept a total of an hour, I felt ground by that leaden heel more than ever. This was our life for the foreseeable future.

I was in the kitchen again and a man rushed in and began putting bags of food on the help-yourself shelf. He asked me if I wanted any. "We're going home," he said, and I said, "That's great." But he replied, "No, our son died today."

His two-year-old son.

He left. I didn't move. Then a woman came in and started boiling bottles. Her new daughter was in the NICU. She'd been born with fluid-filled cysts in her lungs, and the doctors didn't know what to do.

I felt something inside me snap. A delicate bone, a little dried twig. I said to Cito later, "We have to get out of here.

He said, "We are getting out of here." Our discharge date was days away.

But something could happen to delay the date, an infection, anything.

Asa's discharge meeting was held in a conference room near the TCU. Reports were given that summarized all of Asa's history and expectations for the future.

The estimated time for needing the tracheostomy, Dr. Storytime stated, was one to two years. He was a judge reading out a sentence. Still, I was aware that there were many parents who would give anything to be in our position.

We had a chance to thank most of Asa's "team" at that meeting, and they nodded and smiled at us.

Afterward, N. Cheerful showed us Asa's respite schedule for the last days of June. She had found nurses to cover every night of our first week at home, and she was working on July.

N. Elegance said it would take time to transition to being at home. But that the days were going to fly by.

The days would fly by. There might be light and wings. And we'd get through it.

Asa's discharge day did come.

Another friend from California was there to help, and a friend from Vancouver.

My mom had presents for the staff at the TCU and the Haunter House, and there was a little party for Asa in the unit.

It was hectic trying to get everything packed up for Asa, digging our stuff out of the Haunter House, getting the frozen milk from the NICU. If I'd been in the habit of biting my nails, I would have gone down to the knuckles. I was sure something would foil our escape.

YOU'RE GOING TO HAVE SO MUCH FUN WITH HER!

GOOD BYE

GOOD BYE

GOOD LUCK

THANK YOU

THANK YOU

GOOD BYE

In the parking lot we discovered my mom hadn't yet hooked up the car seat and didn't know how.

Luckily, a car-seat-installing volunteer was waiting by the entrance to help new babies go home.

Then we were packed in the car. My mom and our friend in the front and Cito and I in the back with Asa between us. We were leaving, pulling out of the parking lot and away.

Cito and I had come to the hospital for an ultrasound and were leaving with a five-month-old baby. I felt like we were adopting her.

She wasn't going to belong to the hospital anymore. She was to be ours. And Asa, she looked out the window at buildings and trees going by, seemingly unsurprised.

As if the most natural thing in the world were this uncertain adventure.

She was doing so well. She was our star. She was our star.

And we could be together now, in all the things ahead of us.

Epilogue

The first year at home was the hardest, but Asa was doing well. She crawled on time, began eating, started learning sign language and loving stories. She danced at her first birthday party, started walking and soon started throwing up less and less, which was a real blessing. With good luck and help from the breast pump she stayed, for the most part, very healthy. Both western and alternative medicine were our much-needed allies.

Soon after Asa's second birthday a scope showed dramatic improvement in the malacia of her lower trachea, it now being much less collapsible. We were on our way to decannulation (having the trake out) so we thought. But another more thorough scope six months later showed a severe malacia in an upper section.

After this scope the doctors no longer had an estimate for the trake, it was just wait and see. We cancelled our plans for leaving Canada and applied for permanent residence. What we did know, and did have, was that Asa was a growing, happy, healthy, sweet, smart kid. Our blank slate was all possibility.

Asa learned to eat and drink completely by mouth before her third birthday. The G-tube came out and she underwent another surgery to close the site. At this same time the doctors performed another bronchoscopy that showed no improvement whatsoever in her trachea. Dr. Littlebox consulted with colleagues in Cincinnati, the airway specialists in North America. They knew of only a handful of kids with Asa's scenario. For some, the missing cartilage grew in, and for others it didn't. The next window of opportunity for cartilage growth would be between five and seven years of age, and the next one would be puberty. New surgical techniques were developing, and if the cartilage never grew in, Asa might, far down the road, be a candidate for a new procedure.

Life went on and things did get easier. We organized a playgroup so Asa could have peers she saw regularly, but without the usual level of preschool germ exposure. She took a dance class and an art class, had friends, real and imaginary, and while there were some outpatient procedures and ER visits, she was never readmitted to the hospital.

The summer Asa was five, we moved from Vancouver to a small town on Vancouver Island, where Asa started kindergarten. By then, nights were stable and our nursing support switched to school hours, and soon we no longer needed to use the suction machine. Asa loved school. She mastered the monkey bars, and trake or no trake, she had a great life.

When Asa was seven we traveled back to Vancouver for another scope. To the surprise of Dr. Littlebox there was a slight improvement; it appeared a small amount of cartilage had grown in. He said to come back in a year or two.

We moved again, to the city of Victoria, where Asa began the third grade. With each year the trake became less of a big deal. She couldn't swim underwater, and she had to go everywhere with Cito or me or a nurse, but it didn't hold her back. Asa was an excellent student, took martial arts classes, made a wonderful group of friends, fell in love with drama and had a key role in the school play, decided to wear exclusively boys' clothes and now identifies as "gender neutral."

In June of 2015 Asa had another scope. This time everything was different. Her trachea was much improved and we had the green light to go ahead with the steps toward decannulation. On September 21st, after a night of monitoring in the hospital, Asa herself cut the trach tie and removed the tube. She was ten years old and tube-free for the first time.

She's looking forward to swimming lessons.

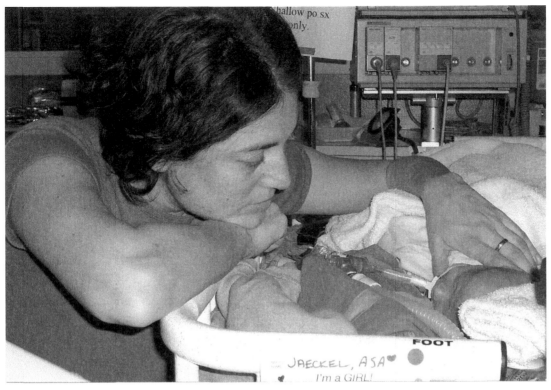

Asa and Jenny
March 2005

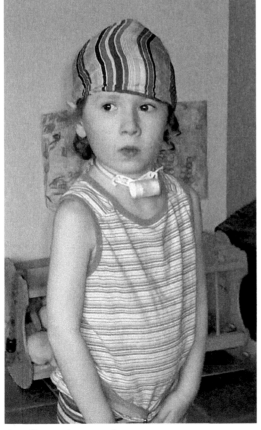

Asa, December 2008

Asa, December 2015

acknowledgements

To the many friends, family member and health professionals who have helped us, my deepest possible thanks.

Many thanks for the generous support and feedback of: Susan Steudel, Melody Kimmel, Teresa Goff, Chris O'Connor, Scott Malin, Cindy Mochizuki, Brett Warnock, and especially Josue Menjivar, this project's patron saint. Many additional thanks to the Xeric Foundation, for the generous grant that financed the publication of the first edition of this book.

Finally, thank you Erika Lunder of Raincloud Press and Rita Arciniega, for your wonderful collaboration on this new edition and its translation for the Spanish version.